THE SHROPSHIRE UNION CANAL

Brewood to Market Drayton

Mike Cope

First published in Great Britain in 2013

British Library Cataloguing-in-Publication Data
A CIP record for this title is available from the British Library

ISBN 978 0 85710 077 1

PiXZ Books
Halsgrove House, Ryelands Business Park,
Bagley Road, Wellington, Somerset TA21 9PZ
Tel: 01823 653777
Fax: 01823 216796
email: sales@halsgrove.com

An imprint of Halstar Ltd, part of the Halsgrove group of companies
Information on all Halsgrove titles is available at:
www.halsgrove.com

Printed and bound in China by
Toppan Leefung Printing Ltd

Acknowledgement

The author would like to thank Peter Gillard for historical information and Rob Cope for assistance with photography.

Contents

	How to use this book	4
1	Brewood	7
2	Lapley and Wheaton Aston	13
3	High Onn and Church Eaton	19
4	Cowley and Wood Eaton	25
5	Gnosall and Doley Common	31
6	Norbury Junction	37
7	Loynton Moss and Grub Street	43
8	Shebdon, Knighton and High Offley	47
9	Goldstone and Cheswardine	53
10	Market Drayton and Tyrley Locks	59

How to use this book

The Area

The Shropshire Union Canal runs from the outskirts of Wolverhampton to Ellesmere Port, covering a distance of some 66 miles, and falling more than 300 feet, down 44 locks. The "Shroppie", as it is affectionately known, is a "union" of three canals: the Birmingham & Liverpool Junction Canal, the Chester Canal and the Ellesmere Canal (Wirral line).The Birmingham & Liverpool Junction Canal (from Autherley Junction to Nantwich) was the last great narrow boat canal to be built and is a product of the later period of canal construction.

On 22 September 1825, a meeting was convened at the Royal Victoria Hotel, Newport by the Canal Committee, to raise support for the new venture, and in May 1826 an Act of Parliament was passed authorising the building of the canal, with Thomas Telford as the principal engineer.

Eschewing the contour-hugging characteristics of previous waterways, Telford favoured the 'cut and fill' technique – digging deep cuttings through the hills and carting away the spoil to build embankments over the valleys. This method of construction enabled a more direct route across country – with long lock-free sections (or pounds) to reduce journey times – and anticipated the methodology later used by the railway engineers.

However, it was considerably more difficult to raise a water channel 60 feet above the surrounding area, than to lay a railway line in the same place. The chasm-like cuttings at Woodseaves and Grub Street are deep, man-made canyons, dug without the aid of mechanisation, with pick and shovel, and subject to recurrent rock falls. The massive Shelmore embankment, near Norbury – over a mile long and containing over a million cubic feet of earth – gave Telford enormous difficulties with frequent slippages, and took a troublesome 5½ years to build.

The Birmingham & Liverpool Junction Canal finally opened to traffic on

2 March 1835, at a cost of £800,000, and soon became an efficient and economical means of transporting goods. In 1870, over a third of the company's fleet of 213 horse-drawn narrow boats were employed in the carriage of iron ore and finished metal goods. Other staple cargoes, that plied their way along the Shroppie, were coal, limestone, grain, milk, cheese and chocolate crumb.

In 1939, L.T.C. Rolt made his 'dream-like' visit along the Midlands canals, and devoted three chapters of his iconic book, *Narrow Boat*, to the stretch between Market Drayton and the 'cut end' at Autherley Junction.

As the working narrow boats slowly disappeared, a new form of waterway traffic emerged and the canal became a firm favourite with pleasure boaters. The main line was nationalized in 1947 and assured of a long term future (by its present owners British Waterways), when it was designated a 'Cruiseway' in 1968.

Routes and Maps

The Shroppie falls 40 feet (down six locks) between Brewood (bridge 11) and Market Drayton (bridge 62) – a distance of approx. 23 miles. The canal bridges are numbered sequentially in the direction of flow and the walking routes follow the same convention, beginning in the southernmost section.

All walks are circular, ranging from 3 - 7 miles and are graded from one to three boots – from easy to the more challenging. Conveniently, the whole area is covered by the 242 and 243 OS Explorer maps.

Further Reading

Shropshire Union Canal Cruising Guide (Autherley Junction to Ellesmere Port), Waterways World, 1991.

The Shroppie, Thomas Pellow and Paul Bowen, The Landscape Press, 1985.

Thomas Telford, L.T.C. Rolt, Penguin, 1985 (first published 1958).

Narrow Boat, L.T.C. Rolt, Alan Sutton Publishing, 1994 (first published 1944).

Key to Symbols Used

Level of difficulty:

Easy ♥

Fair ♥♥

More challenging ♥♥♥

Map symbols:

Park & start

Walk route

Road

Canal/water

Building

Church

Pub

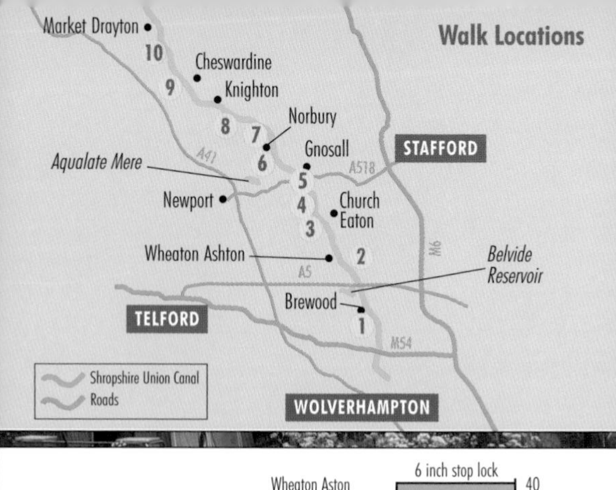

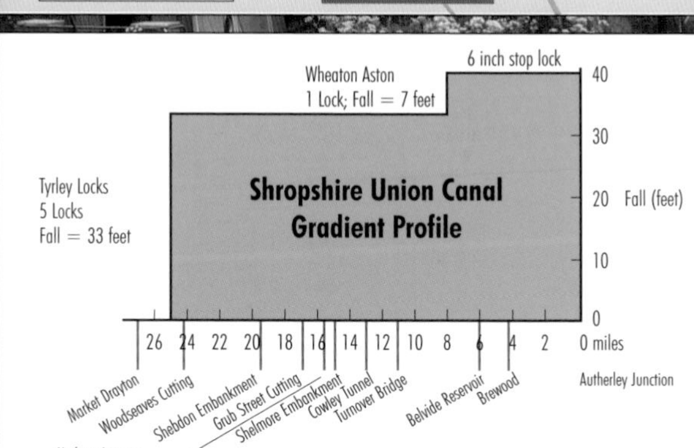

1 Brewood

Explore the southern end of the Shroppie near its source, on this 5 ¼ mile circuit.

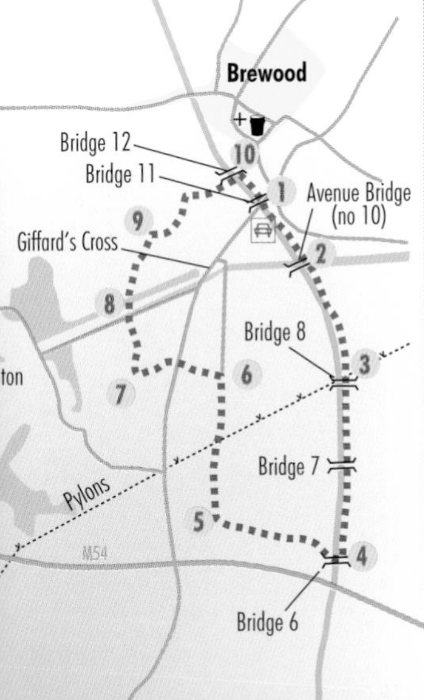

Autherley Junction is where the Shroppie meets the older Staffordshire and Worcestershire canal – built by James Brindley in 1772. A stop lock of only 6 inches was originally installed to divide the two waterways, for fear that the Shroppie might steal their water. The prime purpose of canals was transportation, and the fastest way to ship goods was by fly boat, which covered the distance from Birmingham to Ellesmere Port in a mere 29 hours. These ran to a strict timetable, with fresh horses being supplied at strategic change-over points (Autherley Junction, Norbury Junction and Tyrley).

Level:
Length: 5 ¼ miles (8.3 km)
Terrain: After leaving canal towpath, easy walking along linear tracks and field paths.
Park and start: Layby near bridge 11, Brewood.
Start ref: SJ 885080
Postcode (nearest): ST19 9DF
Public transport: None to start, but Arriva bus 76 from Stafford to Wolverhampton stops in Brewood.
Refreshments and facilities: The Admiral Rodney pub, Brewood.

1 From the lay-by, descend the flight of steps, with wooden handrail, to join canal towpath at **bridge 11**. Bear left along towpath with huge sycamore trees on both banks that tilt inwards towards centre of canal.

Narrow boat moored near bridge 11.

Pass under the **Avenue Bridge (no. 10)** which has

The Avenue Bridge (no. 10).

ornamental balustrades across the top, giving a clue to its origin. The route across the bridge leads to Chillington Hall, and it is likely that the landowner would have only allowed the canal to cross his land, if its commercial nature could be suitably disguised. If you wish to view the balustrades at close quarters, make a short diversion up the wooden staircase to left of bridge. To continue the walk, keep ahead along the canal towpath towards **bridge 9**. A flotilla

Narrow boat about to enter bridge 8.

of canal boats and landing stages/ pontoons can be seen on the opposite bank, where the canal widens into a basin. Very soon the towpath leaves behind the tree cover and fields can be seen on both sides of the canal.

The ornate Avenue Bridge (no. 10) was built to placate the Giffard family, whose tree-lined avenue to Chillington Hall was pierced by the canal.

Boaters exchange greetings.

3 Just before **bridge 8**, the buzzing of power lines can be heard high above the canal, and beyond it there is another long, linear section of canal, with boats moored on the nearside bank. If you come in summer, you may see a combine harvester threshing corn in one of

Cast iron milepost between bridges 7 and 8.

the adjacent fields. Pass a milestone indicating that Autherley Junction – where the Shroppie forms a junction with the Staffordshire and Worcestershire Canal – is only 3 miles away, and in the direction you are heading! Just after **bridge 7**, pass a brick bunker, used to store stop planks to dam the canal. You may be lucky enough to see a heron wading out into the shallows, and then flying off, if disturbed, with slow wing beats. Teasel and Rosebay Willowherb also adorn this section of the towpath in summertime. Listen out for a faint roar, which grows progressively louder – which is the **M54 motorway** up ahead! Continue along towpath in a straight and linear line towards the next **bridge (no. 6)**.

Baled hay and Wolverhampton tower blocks.

4 Just before you reach it, leave the towpath and join a track that runs parallel to it. Bear right over bridge and continue along tarred lane. The route passes through **Old Hatton Farm**, with its white farm buildings, and then proceeds along a dead straight section of road, which would be the envy of any Roman road builder! The road appears to be concrete (not tarmac) and to have been made in short sections – like an airport runway! Ignore the next turning right, and proceed up the hill. Near the top, look left for glimpses of cars on the M54 motorway - well screened from the surrounding landscape by a cutting. Beyond it, the tower blocks of Wolverhampton and its suburbs, can be seen in the far distance.

5 When you reach a **circular road mirror** near crest of hill, bear right along road past a strip of conifer and broadleaf woodland. When the drive swings left into a farm, keep ahead along unmade road. Again this track is long and linear, which seems to be a characteristic of the walk. Pass under **power lines**, where the air crackles around the live wires. When you reach the crest of the hill, proceed along a wooded avenue and then through a swing gate. Continue along hedged path, towards houses and a tarred lane.

6 Bear left along hedged lane with no footpath. Take care should you meet any approaching cars – although it is unlikely that you will. At the main road, go straight across along driveway. When driveway ends, keep ahead along footpath which, in due course, swings round to the left.

7 Take the first right through wooden kissing gate to join the **Staffordshire Way**. Follow the narrow ribbon of footpath along right hand edge of field and past two **dried-up pits**. Go through gate at end of field and then across tarred lane and through another wooden gate.

The Staffordshire Way is a 92 mile long distance footpath that runs from Mow Cop, on the edge of the Peak District, to Kinver Edge, near Stourbridge.

In the 19th century, lime-rich marl was dug from marl pits and spread on the land to improve the alkalinity and soil structure. The pit holes were then filled with ground-water and used as watering holes for livestock.

Giffard's Cross (near bridge 11) marks the spot where Sir John Giffard reputedly shot dead a panther with a bow and arrow, in the early 16th century, which had escaped from Brewood forest.

8 Continue along the **Staffordshire Way** and across a driveway to **Chillington Hall**. Go through metal kissing gate and proceed along right hand edge of next field. When fence runs out, maintain direction along line of hawthorns to gate at end of field.

View of Brewood church from bridge 12.

9 Go right along untarred lane, past a three-storey **farm house**, where track swings gradually round to the left. When you reach a T-junction, go right past a cream **pebble-dashed cottage**, and keep going until you reach a bridge over the canal (no.12).

10 Bear left down concrete steps to join the canal towpath. If you wish to make a diversion to **Brewood village** (recommended), go right though metal gate and aim for church spire. To continue walk, go left under bridge, and proceed to next bridge **(no. 11)**. Pass under bridge, and then climb wooden staircase back to layby where the walk began.

Narrow boat about to enter bridge 12.

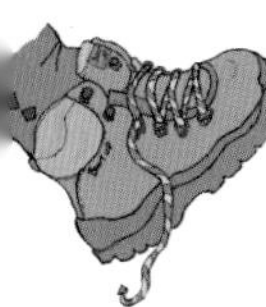

2 **Lapley and Wheaton Aston**

An exhilarating 7 mile hike that takes in a reservoir, originally built as the principal water source for the Shroppie.

Belvide Reservoir is a 180 acre man-made reservoir, built in the 1830s, as the principal water source for the Shropshire Union Canal. It is now a nature reserve and an SSSI designated site, operated by the West Midland Bird Club, the UK's largest regional ornithological society. In recent years, the principal water source for the canal has come from the very head of the canal itself (at Autherley Junction). The nearby Barnhurst sewage works has been pumping up to 12 million gallons of purified effluent a day into the canal.

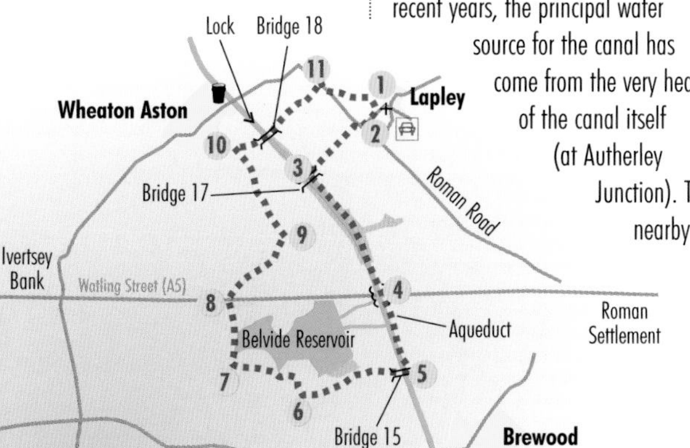

Level:

Length: 7 miles (11.2 km)

Terrain: Easy walking along towpath and across fields. Some road walking involved between canal and reservoir.

Park and start: Pull-in near All Saints church, Lapley.

Start ref: SJ 872129

Postcode (nearest): ST19 9JS

Public transport: Arriva bus 3 from Wolverhampton stops in Lapley.

Refreshments and facilities: The Hartley Arms, Wheaton Aston; Homestead Caravan Park, Leisure Club.

1 Locate entrance to **All Saints church, Lapley** and then continue along churchyard wall towards yellow cottage. At the first corner, go right at fingerpost and continue along left hand edge of field. If you come in summer, you'll see a long line of blackthorn bushes, heavy laden with sloes. If you look half right, you'll see the whale-back outline of **The Wrekin** in the distance. In due course, the path drops down to a T-junction, near a road.

All Saints church, Lapley.

Field of cows near Lapley.

2 Go right here, and when you reach the road, go straight across along a tarred lane **(The Staffordshire Way)**. Pass some lime trees and then a small holding on the left. When the lane ends, continue through farmyard, aiming for a pile of tyres. Before you reach it, bear half left towards a gate.

Farmyard near bridge 17.

3 Go through gate, and then turn left down ramp to gain canal towpath at **bridge 17**. Bear left and continue along a straight section of canal. Pass a **milestone** indicating that it is 7 miles to Autherley Junction and 8 ½ miles to Norbury Junction. In due course, the canal swings to the right in a slow arc, as tall ash trees tilt towards the centre of the canal. It is relatively quiet here, except for pigeons' cooing and the occasional clap of birds' wings in the wood. After the bend, there is another long straight section of waterway, with boats moored on the towpath side.

Narrow boat in Lapley Wood Cutting.

View from towpath near boat maintenance yard.

4 After a boat maintenance yard, the canal narrows to cross **Watling Street (A5)** via Thomas Telford's exquisite **aqueduct**, built in 1832. Pass another milestone post and opposite it, a brick structure,

The Stretton Aqueduct was built by Thomas Telford, in 1832, to carry the canal over Watling Street. The sturdy, but elegant, cast-iron trough is complemented by blue-brick abutments and decorative sandstone columns.

Crossing the Stretton Aqueduct.

which looks like a pillbox. A **feeder channel** from Belvide Reservoir also joins the canal nearby. Go under **bridge 16** and exit the canal at the next **bridge (no. 15)**.

5 Gain the road, and then bear left over bridge. Continue through **Homestead Caravan Park** and past the **leisure club** entrance.

Ignore the next track off to the right, and continue walking along road. Look right to catch a glimpse of the eastern edge of **Belvide Reservoir**.

Pass car park for **Belvide Bird Reserve**, and continue along road. Since there is no footway, remember to walk on the right, facing the approaching traffic, except where it's safer to walk on the left (i.e. at a right hand bend). The road walking may seem interminable, but – take heart – it will end soon!

6 Take the next right, along a farm track to **Birks Barn Farm**. Pass a white farmhouse on the left and continue to end of lane. Go left through gate and across corn field,

The V Festival was the first UK festival to operate a two site option and swap line-ups overnight. Since 1999, Weston Park became the new home for the V festival in the North and some of the world's greatest bands and solo artists have performed here.

aiming for **pocket of woodland**. Look right here to see **Belvide Reservoir** glistening through the trees. If you come in mid August, you may hear the distant strains of the V-Festival, emanating from the nearby Weston Park. Enter woodland, go through gate, and then cross a small wooden foot-bridge. Continue through woodland glade, and along narrow path, with large conifers on the left. Go through another gate and along a path through middle of cornfield. Pass along left hand edge of woodland, and follow track as it swings round to the right towards a farm. When you reach a field (before the farm), aim for wooden gate in the top right hand corner.

7 Turn right along untarred lane, past two small horse chestnut trees. Very soon, you'll reach a strip of grass, near a low fence, which is an excellent place to stop and admire **Belvide Reservoir**, with its flocks of water fowl. Behind the reservoir, on the distant horizon, you can also make out **Pye Green Tower** on Cannock Chase. Continue along lane, and when you reach the main road **(A5)**, bear left.

8 After 50 metres, go right across road and along bridle-way. Go through two gates and then across **farmyard**, aiming for pile of tyres. Go through third gate and proceed along right hand edge of field (which may contain geese). Go through another gate and continue along right hand edge of large field. Go through gate at end of field with farm on right – a field's breadth back.

Belvide Reservoir.

9 Bear half left across corn field along the obvious path, which leads to a gate and a wooded lane. Go immediately left through gate and across another corn field. Go through galvanized gate at end of field, and maintain direction along farm track, which is hedged on both sides. Pass hard standing on right and continue along lane which starts descending gradually.

10 When you reach a gap in the hedge, near a wooden finger-post, bear right across a field and under two sets of **powerlines**. Go

The single lock at Wheaton Aston marks the start of the long unbroken 17 mile pound to Tyrley.

The one-time Priory church of All Saints, Lapley stands on high ground and its tower is a conspicuous landmark. The reason for the structural misalignment of chancel and nave is unknown. Some of the headstones in the nearby cemetery have touching and original epitaphs.

through wooden kissing gate, and across next field, and then through three gates in quick succession, before crossing **bridge over canal (no.18)**. If you wish to make a diversion to the Hartley Arms pub, Wheaton Aston, go left along towpath, towards lock and get off at next bridge (no. 19). To continue the walk, keep ahead down wooden steps and across corn field,

Footbridge near Lapley.

aiming for large oak tree. Proceed along right hand edge of next field. When hedge swings right, keep ahead towards metal gate at end of field (to the left of church tower). Climb stile and proceed across meadow (which may contain cattle) to another stile and over **concrete footbridge**.

11 Cross road and then bear right along it. Take the next left along **Church Lane** and keep going until you reach **Lapley church**, where the walk began.

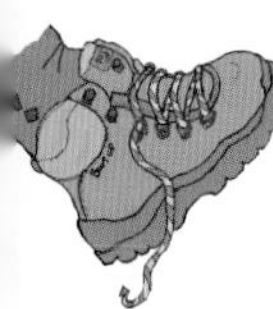

3 High Onn and Church Eaton

A challenging 6 ¼ mile circuit that takes in a former canal wharf, a World War II airfield and a 12th century church.

Level: 3 of 3
Length: 6 ¼ miles (10.2 km)
Terrain: After leaving canal towpath, a varied and challenging route along rarely-used field paths.
Park and start: Pull-in at Turnover Bridge (no.26).
Start ref: SJ 832172
Postcode (nearest): ST20 0AY (1km away)
Public transport: None to start, but Arriva bus 482 from Stafford to Marston stops in Church Eaton.
Refreshments and facilities: The Royal Oak pub, Church Eaton.

St Editha's is an impressive 12th century church, dominated by a magnificent east window with 19th century glass by Kempe in ancient tracery. Local tradition suggests that the stonework (for this window) was brought up from St Paul's Cathedral after the Great Fire of 1666. However, it is more likely to have come from one of the three Stafford religious houses after their dissolution in 1538. The spectacular spire, which can be seen for miles, was added in the 15th century and heightened in 1879.

The churchyard has won numerous gold and silver awards in the diocesan best kept churchyard competition.

Wood Eaton
Church Eaton
Apeton
…ver Bridge (n…o. 26)
1
2
3
4
5
6
7
8
9
10
11
12
Bridge 24
Bridge 23
…Onn …arf
…dge 25
Little Onn
Edith's Well
Church Eaton Brook
Little Onn Airfield (disused)

1 Go through gate and down ramp to gain canal towpath at the **Turnover Bridge (no. 26)**. Bear left and continue along canal, past moored craft on opposite bank. All moorings have landing stages and access for cars along driveway on upper level. Proceed past **High Onn Wharf**, and under **bridge 25**. Continue along straight section of canal with boats moored on both banks. Their names give clues to their owner's intentions: *Narrow Escape, Second Chance, Panacea, Bliss, Nirvana, Great Escape,* – to name but a few.

A roving or turnover bridge enabled a horse to cross the canal, when the towpath changed sides, without the need to unhitch the towline.

The Turnover Bridge (no. 26).

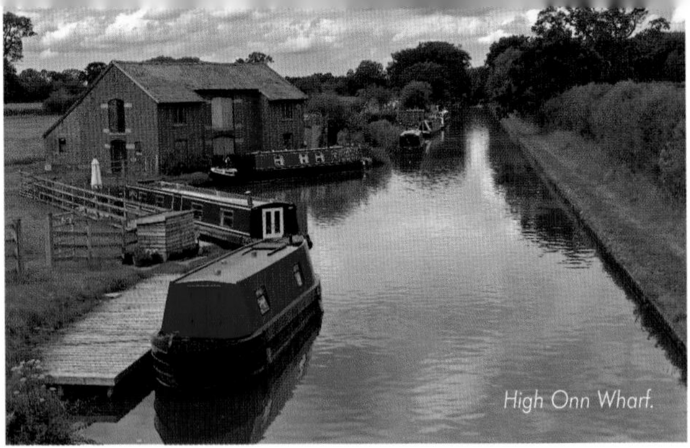

High Onn Wharf.

High Onn Wharf once served the nearby village of Church Eaton with a quay for handling cargoes and a two-storey red-brick warehouse for storing goods. It is used today as a winding hole (or turning point) for 72 ft craft.

St Edith's Well is situated on private land near High Onn bridge, and is traditionally believed to possess healing properties (for eye disorders). The 'well' is a chamber about 5 feet deep with access to the water via stone steps.

Pass under **bridge 24**, and continue along a linear section of canal. After passing a milestone post, the canal plunges into a wooded cutting (Rye Hill) and begins to swing round to the right.

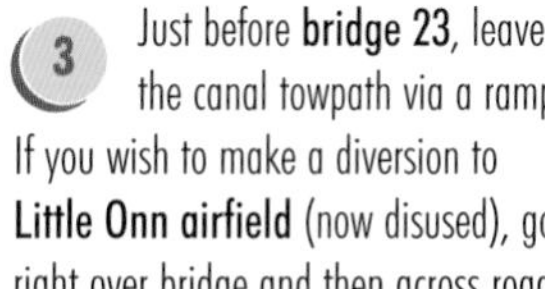

Just before **bridge 23**, leave the canal towpath via a ramp. If you wish to make a diversion to **Little Onn airfield** (now disused), go right over bridge and then across road. To continue walk, bear left away from bridge, through gate and across field (of maize). Half way across field, Pye Green Tower, Cannock Chase is visible, on the distant horizon. At end of field, maintain direction across next field, keeping hedge on right. Join farm track at end of field and proceed to a road.

RAF Wheaton Aston was established at Little Onn in 1941 and used as a training school for American pilots. When the aerodrome was abandoned in 1947, the converted huts were used (for another 18 years) as a Polish resettlement camp, and then as a British-Polish housing estate.

Cross road and maintain direction along track. Pass

Rye Hill Cutting.

Sheep near Woollaston Farm.

through belt of woodland with pit on right. Soon after, the lane becomes overgrown, but can be traversed without difficulty. Go through metal gate, where track is hedged on both sides, and the going gets easier. Strawberries are often grown under cloches in the field to your right. Pass farm buildings on right and then go through a gate. Follow track as it veers sharply left and then continues to a road.

5 Turn right and then immediately left (opposite farm) along bridleway. After a few hundred metres, go right through gate along edge of field. Before you reach field corner, cut left towards wooden gate in top left hand corner of field. Cross stream via gated footbridge, and maintain direction across next field. The waymarking here is virtually non-existent, which might explain why the paths are seldom used (until now that is)! Go through metal gate and along left hand edge of next field to another gate. Maintain direction along farm track and past pit on right. Go through a further gate and then proceed along hedged lane. The quality of the track seems to have evolved in small increments over the last half mile or so.

6 After 200 metres, bear left through metal gate (bearing a blue arrow) and continue across corn field, aiming for large oak tree. Follow narrow path to a gate and then proceed along sinuous path through **Shredicote Wood**. Cross stream and when you emerge from woodland, continue along right hand edge of next field. You should now be able to see the spire of Church Eaton church, across the fields to your left. Keep going along grassy bank, until it merges with a farm track. Proceed past **pit**, surrounded by poplars with heart-shaped leaves, that shake in the wind.

7 Turn left when you reach a road, and then right (100 metres later) across field and along

Fenced ditch near Apeton.

right hand edge of **pit**. At end of pit, locate waymarked post and proceed in direction of yellow arrow. Climb stile at end of field and proceed along left hand edge of next field. Cross foot-bridge with stile at each end and repeat the same procedure at the end of next field. Pass pit on left, climb stile and continue along left hand edge of field. When it ends, go left over stile and along right hand edge of next field. Soon afterwards, turn right through double gate and proceed along farm track. Continue through **farmyard**, past cattle sheds and along tarred drive.

8 Turn left at road, pass village sign and then cross bridge over stream. 100 metres before you reach the wall of **St Editha's Church, Church Eaton**, there is a stile and a

Spire of St Editha's, Church Eaton.

Detail of window in St Editha's Church.

fingerpost. Keep ahead if you wish to visit the church (recommended).

9 To continue walk, bear half right right over stile and along narrow enclosed path. Climb stile and proceed across field to another stile. Continue along left hand edge of large field, past the back of the village school and its playing fields. When you reach field corner, go right along top edge of field, and then left over gate and along drive. If you wish to make a diversion to the **Royal Oak pub**, turn left when you reach the road.

10 To continue the walk, go right along road, and then take the next bridleway on the left.

11 When you reach a junction, branch left down a hedged track. Duck under a metal pole and proceed along narrow path through woodland, with large pits on both sides. Climb stile and continue along left hand edge of field to another stile.

12 Turn right along road and branch right at next fork (Joan Eaton's Cross). Keep going until you reach the **Turnover Bridge (no. 26)**, where the walk began.

The Turnover Bridge in late May.

4 Cowley and Wood Eaton

A tunnel hewn from solid sandstone, a cavernous cutting and two canalside pubs are all on offer on this 4 ¾ mile ramble.

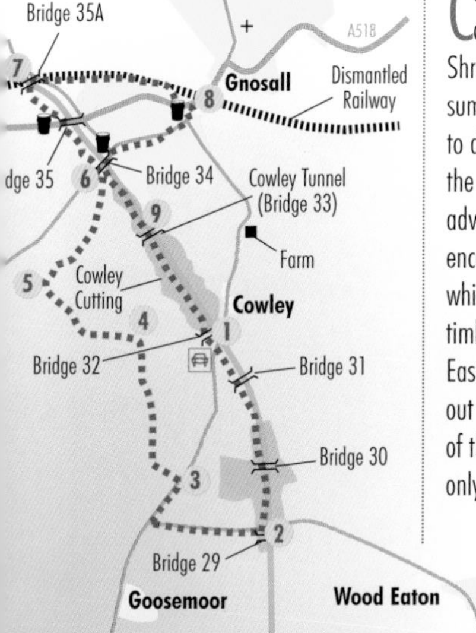

Cowley Tunnel has the distinction of being the only one on the Shropshire Union main line. In the summer of 1830, the miners began to drive the tunnel at Cowley, from the northern end, but had only advanced ninety yards when they encountered badly faulted rock, which had to be shored up with timbering. After consultation, Telford, Easton and Provis decided to open out the remainder as a cutting and of the 690 yards originally planned, only 81 yards remained as a tunnel.

Level:

Length: 4 ¾ miles (7.7 km)

Terrain: Easy walking along towpath, quiet country lanes and field paths.

Park and start: Pull-in at Cowley Bridge (no.32).

Start ref: SJ 828192

Postcode (nearest): ST20 0BE

Public transport: None to start, but Arriva bus 481 from Stafford to Telford stops at the The Royal Oak pub, Gnosall (near point 8).

Refreshments and facilities: Pubs in Gnosall (The Boat Inn; The Navigation; The Royal Oak).

High arched bridge (no. 30).

1 Cross road and proceed down ramp to join the canal towpath. Maintain direction towards **bridge 31**, with fields on both sides of canal. Note the **cast-iron rubbing plates**, which have been worn down by the ropes of horse-drawn barges. Continue past an overflow to the canal on the far bank, and then a **milepost**, which indicates that Autherley Junction is 13 miles away and Norbury Junction 3 ½ miles, in the opposite direction. Pass under a high-arched **bridge (no. 30)** covered in moss, with ferns growing out of the stonework. Continue along a straight, muddy section of towpath, which always seems to bear the imprint of bike tyres.

Cast-iron rubbing plates were affixed to all bridges shortly after the canal opened, to stop tow-ropes cutting into the stonework. A wet rope collects grit, and makes it abrasive to sandstone.

2 Pass under **Wood Eaton Bridge (no.29)**, and then bear right up ramp to gain the road. Turn left along lane that carries little

Wood Eaton Bridge (no. 29).

The road to Gnosall.

traffic – except farm vehicles – and has grass growing down the centre. If you come in August , don't be surprised to see a combine cutting corn in the surrounding fields. The hedgerows here are ancient, and consist of hawthorn, oak, hazel, ash and elderberry. Pass a **dried-up pit**, surrounded by poplars, and when you reach a **T-junction**, bear right along the Gnosall road.

3 Take the next left (at the fingerpost) up a farm track, and when you reach a galvanized gate, go right over stile and along left hand edge of field. Continue along a wide walkway, and when it veers sharp right, go left over two rickety stiles. Cross two further fields (both with stiles), and then continue across a short strip of grassland. Cross a wooden footbridge with stiles at both ends, and then traverse another field – aiming for a galvanised gate to the left of a large tree.

4 Climb a high stile and then go left along a farm track **(Fan Lizard Lane)**. When lane ends, bear right at fingerpost across field, following the obvious path.

Crossing a corn field.

5 At end of field, go right, aiming for large oak tree. Keep ahead along well-worn path maintained by local farmer. Climb stile in field corner and proceed down narrow hedged path. This was once called

The Boat Bridge (no. 34).

Lazards Lane, and suggests there may have been a leper colony here, in bygone times. Pass a pit and a field of goats, and when the path ends, keep ahead along **Quarry Lane**.

6 Just before the the **Boat Bridge (no. 34)**, go down ramp to join canal towpath and bear left along it. Continue under the **A 518 road bridge (no. 35)** and past

Coton Mill and bridge 35.

Coton Steam Mill was built in the 1830s, after the canal was completed, and ground corn grown by local farmers and supplied them with feed for livestock. It passed to a firm of grocers around 1900 and later became Walwyn's shop.

The Navigation pub and **Coton Mill** (now a private residence). Pass under **bridge 35A** – built to carry the railway over the canal – and then bear left up flight of steps to join the **Stafford to Newport Greenway**.

7 Go left along the former dismantled railway, with fields on the left and houses on the right (Glendower Estate). Cross a road bridge **(Willey Lane)** and then look left for views over the allotments towards **Gnosall Village** and **St Lawrence's church**. Eventually the path veers right past **Gnosall Chippy Jumps** (a BMX bike course) and then left (opposite **Gnosall Fish Bar**) to join the main road **(A518)**.

8 Cross road and continue to the **Royal Oak pub**, and then bear right up **Wharf Road**. Pass **Gnosall fire station, Fountain House** and two ancient cottages made from local sandstone. Proceed

Fountain House and cottages.

Over the last 150 years the area now occupied by Waterside Court has had many uses. It has been a brickworks, a sawmill, a creamery, a council laboratory and a depot for road grit.

past **The Rank** and cross road before **Gnosall bakery** to continue on opposite footpath. Pass **Monks Walk**, **Impstones** and a parade of shops before veering left over the **Boat Bridge (no. 34)**. Go left over stile and down ramp to join canal towpath. Maintain direction past waterside apartments with narrow boats moored on both sides of the canal.

9 Before you reach **Cowley Tunnel (bridge 33)**, there is a sheer sandstone rock-face on the towpath side and bare exposed sandstone on the opposite bank. Proceed through the 81 yards of unlined tunnel, hewn from Keuper sandstone. The far end has been re-built in recent times, but the main structure still exhibits a hand-carved, rough-hewn appearance. When you emerge, proceed along a steep-sided wooded cutting, with vegetation, foliage and saplings covering its near-vertical sides. Pass under **Cowley Bridge (no.32)**, then leave towpath via ramp, and continue to the pull-in, where the walk began.

The spectacular chasm-like cutting at Cowley was cleared of vegetation and overhanging tree roots in the mid-1980s, because of concerns over the stability of the cut-away rock face.

Emerging from Cowley Tunnel.

Cruising along Cowley Cutting.

5 Gnosall and Doley Common

A diverse 4 ¼ mile circuit that includes a dismantled railway, a canal aqueduct and an extensive marsh.

Doley Common is a linear depression running north-west of Gnosall village, which was caused by retreating glaciers at the end of the last Ice Age. This glacial overflow channel is now an extensive marsh, with peat several metres deep in places. Some years ago workers installing a new storm drain discovered the head and antlers of an Irish Elk or Giant Deer (Megaloceros giganteus) – one of the largest deer that ever lived.

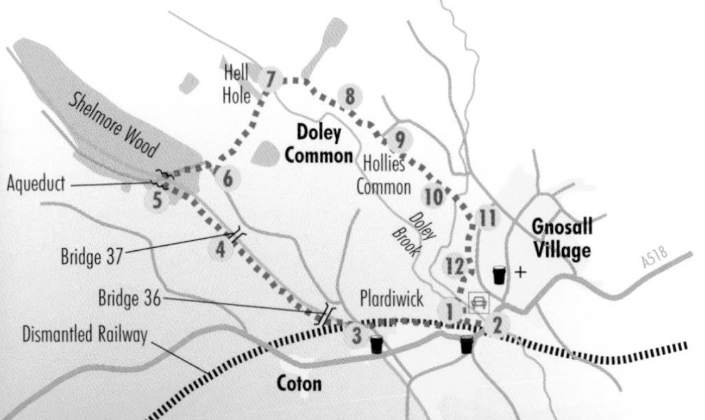

Level: 🥾🥾
Length: 4 ¼ miles (6.7 km)
Terrain: Doley Common can get very waterlogged – walking boots essential.
Park and start: Gnosall allotments car park.
Start ref: SJ 825206
Postcode (nearest): ST20 0BL
Public transport: Arriva bus 481 from Stafford to Telford stops at the Royal Oak pub, Gnosall (300 metres from start of walk).
Refreshments and facilities: Pubs in Gnosall (The Royal Oak; The Navigation; The Boat Inn; The Horns).

The Royal Oak pub, Gnosall.

1 Exit the **Gnosall allotments car park** and proceed along approach road towards the main road **(A518)**. Just before you reach it, go right up flight of wooden steps and through a swing gate, to join the **Stafford to Newport Greenway** (formerly the route of the Stafford to Newport dismantled railway).

The Stafford to Newport Greenway follows the route of the former railway, which was in service for 115 years from 1849 until 1964, when the last steam train plied its way along the line, carrying a wreath to mourn its passing.

Gnosall appeared in the Domesday Book as 'Geneshall', and was part of the West Cuttlestone Hundred. It is the only UK place-name beginning with a silent 'G'.

2 Proceed along embankment, and maintain direction at first junction along wider gravel path **(National Cycle Network 55)**. Look right here for views across the allotments to **Gnosall village** and **St Lawrence church**. In due course, fields will appear on the right and houses on the left **(Glendower Estate)**. Proceed along embanked gravel path with trees and vegetation on both sides. Cross bridge over Plardiwick road and then 200 metres later, go right down flight of steps with wooden handrail to join **canal towpath** near **bridge 35A**.

3 Bear left along canal towpath towards Plardiwick (Leeks) **bridge (no.36)** and then continue

Narrow boat moored near bridge 35A.

Summer evening near Plardiwick.

along a linear stretch of canal to **bridge 37**. Look left here (on a clear day) for views of **The Wrekin**, 15

Canoeist approaching Barns Bridge.

miles away to the west. You may be fortunate enough to see a heron, on the opposite bank, standing stock still, waiting for fish.

4 The canal embankment here is also an idyllic spot to catch the evening sun. The farm to your right **(near bridge 37)** is called Barns Bridge.

The edge of Doley Common.

5 When you reach a disused lock gate and a small concrete building, go left down steps to join road. Bear right under **aqueduct**, and proceed uphill through **Shelmore Wood**. Pass an exposed sandstone outcrop, which offers clues to the underlying geology of the area. At the crest of the hill, the road bends sharply right near **a cottage**.

6 After 200 metres, go left at fingerpost over stile and proceed along right hand edge of field to another stile. Follow line of oak trees to another stile at end of next field. Pass to the left of a small pit, where there are clear views across **Doley Common** towards farm buildings on opposite hillside. The square turret of **St Lawrence church, Gnosall** is also visible across the marshes. Go under electric fence (near overgrown stile), and proceed downhill to another stile. The area to your left is called **Hell**

Plotting a course for Hell Hole.

The intriguingly-named Hell Hole is a glacial kettle hole left in the sediment, following the last Ice Age; it is likely to be caused by the same glacial overflow channel that formed Doley Common.

Hole – a kettle hole, left here from the last Ice Age.

7 Proceed across marsh, and under power lines, to wooden gate. This area can get extremely muddy in wet weather, if **Doley Brook** has burst it banks, so take care and come suitably equipped. Go through second wooden gate, and then bear left through galvanized metal gate and continue along other side of hedge towards belt of woodland. Follow hedgerow as it bends round to right to a double stile. Proceed along right hand edge of field to another (unusually high) stile. The marshland of **Doley Common** should now be on your right hand side, beyond the wire fence. Continue across short field to another stile and then over a small footbridge. Proceed along narrow enclosed path through woodland, which eventually merges with a tarred lane.

8 Continue along lane with houses on both sides **(Hollies Common)**. When road swings sharp left, go right through gate into private driveway **(Timbersbrook cottage)**, and then immediately left over stile.

9 After 30 metres climb a two-step stile and maintain direction along other side of hedge. Look right for superb views of **The Wrekin** and **Lilleshall Monument**. Climb stile at end of field and continue along right hand edge of next field – which may contain some overzealous bullocks! Descend into hollow (where there is a break in the hedge) and maintain direction uphill, aiming for

Cornfield with The Wrekin behind.

At one time (when the village population was considerably smaller) Gnosall had eight pubs: The Boat Inn, The Navigation, The Horns, The Royal Oak, The Romping Cat, The Duke's Head, The Anchor and the Fountain Inn.

large tree. Climb stile and continue along path on other side of hedge.

10 Keep ahead at end of field, climb stile and cross meadow, aiming for second telegraph pole. Go through large metal gate and over small stream to follow yellow waymark along left hand edge of field. Pass under powerlines (with pit on right hand side) and aim for stile at end of field.

11 Go right along tarred path (with concrete fence made of gravel boards on left). Keep on right hand footpath into **Shelmore Way** and when road swings sharply left, keep ahead into **Knightley Way**. After a few hundred metres, path veers left in a slow sweeping arc to follow direction of driveway on lower level.

12 Before you reach **Brookhouse Road**, go right through parking area, with children's play area and **recreation ground** on left. Continue across the Acres, past man-made **pond** and **Doley Brook** floodplain, and along boardwalk to allotments car park, where the walk began.

St Lawrence church, Gnosall.

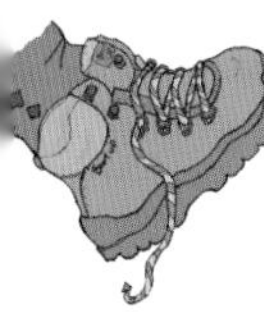

6 Norbury Junction

A fascinating 4 ½ mile walk that combines a classic canal junction with one of the last great engineering feats of the canal building era.

Level:
Length: 4 ½ miles (7.4 km)
Terrain: Easy walking along canal tow-path, woodland tracks and field paths.
Park and start: Norbury Junction car park.
Start ref: SJ 793229
Postcode (nearest): ST20 0PN
Public transport: None to start, but Arriva bus 432 and 433 from Stafford stops in Woodseaves.
Refreshments and facilities: The Junction Inn, Norbury.

The construction of Shelmore Great Bank was not part of the original plans for the canal, until a certain Lord Hanson, of Norbury Park, objected to the canal cutting through his prized game preserves at Shelmore Wood. This forced Telford to swing his line westwards, along the low-lying perimeter of the wood, where it had to be raised on a huge embankment 60 feet high and a mile long. This took a troublesome 5 ½ years to build, and involved moving millions of tons of earth from the nearby cuttings at Grub Street and Cowley. Due to frequent landslips, it was the last section of the canal to be completed in 1835.

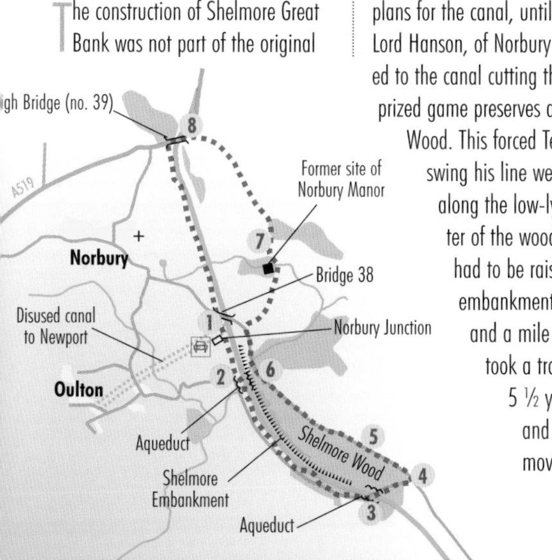

1 Locate the canal towpath and then bear right along it, past the **Junction Inn**. Go over bridge, with a **dry dock** on the right hand side – formerly the route of the now derelict Newport to Shrewsbury Branch. The canal once fell to Newport by a flight of eighteen locks, many of which are now buried underground or deep within wood or scrub growth. Pass an **information centre** and a **British Waterways maintenance yard**, before proceeding along a lofty embankment with boats

Maintenance yard, Norbury Junction.

Tea room and gift shop, Norbury. Junction

A British Waterways canal maintenance yard and section office is based at Norbury Junction. There is also a range of narrow boats for hire, a tea room and a gift shop.

Moorings at Norbury Junction.

A short section of the former Newport to Shrewsbury Branch (closed in 1944) is now used as a dry dock. The Shrewsbury & Newport Canals Trust was set up to preserve the canal's remaining features, with the long term aim of restoring the whole branch line.

moored on both sides. The bluish-grey outline of **The Wrekin** – a prominent local landmark – is also visible on a clear day. From here, you can appreciate just how high the embankment is above the surrounding landscape.

2 The spot where an aqueduct carries the canal across the Norbury to Gnosall road is marked with a wooden fence. If you look

Aqueduct near Norbury Junction.

William Provis successfully tendered for the section between Tyrley and Church Eaton and began work on the Great Shelmore Bank in the late summer of 1829, with a force of 400 men and 70 horses.

Milepost on Shelmore Embankment.

down below, there is a stream that is sourced from the canal overflow. You are now walking along the **Shelmore Great Bank**, which 'caused so much trouble, expense and procrastination' to Telford (and the men who built it) and was not completed until six months after his death. The towpath continues in a slow sweeping arc for another kilometre, before reaching a 'lock gate' and a concrete shack.

3 Go right here down a flight of steps to a road, and then bear right under an **aqueduct**. Continue up a steep bank with woodland on both sides, past an exposed rock face of Keuper sandstone.

When you reach the top of the hill, bear left after a **cottage** and proceed along a wide concrete driveway, with **Shelmore Wood** on the left.

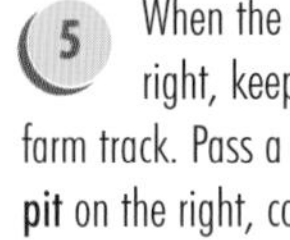

When the driveway swings right, keep ahead along a farm track. Pass a partially dried-up **pit** on the right, covered in green algae. The undulating track becomes more grassed over, with woodland on both sides. In due course, the track emerges from woodland and continues along the left hand edge of a sloping field. Maintain direction as a **gravel drive** merges from the left and eventually joins a road (near the second aqueduct).

In February 1833, a meeting was convened at the Royal Victoria Hotel, Newport to review Provis's section. Following a tour of inspection, the sides of Woodseaves Cutting were cut back further and hardcore tipped at Shelmore to consolidate the bank.

Cottage near Shelmore Wood.

6 Keep ahead along road, past a **row of cottages** and then turn right along a **concrete driveway**. Look left to see the tower of **Norbury church** across the fields, about a kilometre away. Proceed downhill with **cottages and farm buildings**

on the right hand side. The driveway now swings sharply left past a moated platform – once the site of **Norbury Manor**.

7 Leave the concrete drive at the next waymarked junction, and fork left along an unmade road (that runs parallel to powerlines). In due course, the track emerges from woodland with open fields on both sides. On the right, there is a plantation of saplings in plastic tubes, which resembles rows of vines. The track soon becomes fenced on both sides, and then swings sharply left and becomes hedged with a drainage ditch on the left. By and large the walking here is easy; you should have no trouble whatsoever – and could even ride a bike along it! The track then swings right, up a steep bank, before passing a beech tree, where fallen nuts crunch under your feet.

8 When you reach the main road, turn left over the famous **High Bridge (no. 39)** – with its double arch and telegraph pole. Just before a layby, go left through a galvanized gate and down a steep ramp to gain the towpath. Maintain direction along a lush wooded cutting, which contains a variety of trees (ash, sycamore, horse chestnut, elm and beech). This is followed by a long linear section, with narrow boats moored on both sides of the canal. In due course, you will pass under **bridge 38** and arrive at the canal basin, where the walk began.

The lower arch of the famous High Bridge (no. 39) was added later as a strengthening buttress and used as a convenient sitting point for a very short telegraph pole.

High Bridge (no.39).

Craft moored at Norbury Junction.

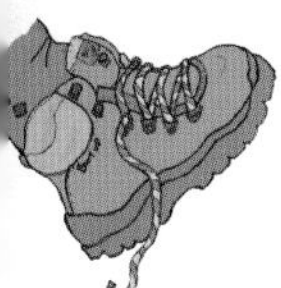

7 Loynton Moss and Grub Street

A 3 mile ramble around a diverse wetland habitat and along one of the Shroppie's great cuttings.

Loynton Moss was formed as a result of glacial action at the end of the last Ice Age. Huge blocks of ice broke from retreating glaciers, gouging a depression known as a kettle hole. When the ice blocks eventually melted, this depression was filled with water to form a mere (Blakemere) that extended more than 100 acres.

Sphagnum moss and natural processes slowly diminished the size of the mere until the last area of open water was lost in the 1950s, to leave an area of fen dominated by tall reed species.

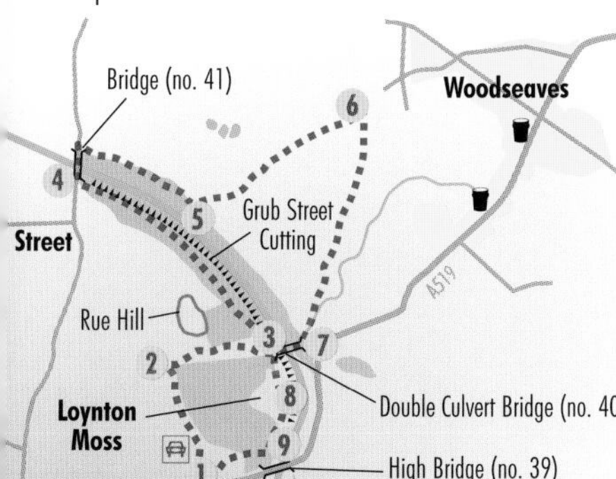

Level:
Length: 3 miles (4.8 km)
Terrain: Easy walking along woodland tracks, canal towpath and field paths.
Park and start: Loynton Moss Nature Reserve car park (300 metres west of the High Bridge, on the A 519).
Start ref: SJ 787242
Postcode (nearest): ST20 0PQ (0.7km away).
Public transport: None to start, but Arriva bus 432 and 433 from Stafford stops in Woodseaves.
Refreshments and facilities: Pubs in Woodseaves (The Cock Inn; The Plough).

(1) Locate information board, and proceed through swing gate and past wooden post with **'Loynton Moss Nature Reserve'** engraved upon it. Cross left hand edge of meadow, go through gate and proceed along track, with woodland on right.

Bluebells at Loynton Moss.

Rue Hill bathed in evening sunlight.

(2) When you reach a T-junction with hillside **(Rue Hill)** behind it, bear right along wide grassy walkway. Fork right at next junction along track which eventually narrows and leads to a swing gate. Go left towards the double culvert bridge, then left again down ramp to join canal towpath at **bridge 40**.

(3) Bear left along **Grub Street Cutting** – a mile long and eighty feet deep. Persistent rock falls caused trouble for the builders, who were forced to open the cutting out to prevent landslips.You might be fortunate enough to see the turquoise dash of a kingfisher, flying low across the water, along this stretch of canal. Pass a **milepost** (indicating that Norbury Junction is only 1½ miles

Cruising through Grub Street Cutting.

away), then an overflow into the canal, and finally a **winding hole**. There may also be craft moored along the towpath edge of the canal at this point.

4 Pass under **bridge 41**, and then go left up ramp to gain road at **Grub Street**. Bear left along road, and when you reach a **white cottage** (after ca.100 metres), go right up steps and over stile into **woodland**. Follow path along edge of wood, keeping the **stream** on your left hand side. Pass a hollowed-out area of woodland with precipitous sides. When the path traverses a sloping bank, take care that you don't loose your footing, twist your ankle or slip into the stream below!

5 Cross stream via **wooden footbridge**, and follow yellow waymark over stile and across field. Pass under **power lines**, climb

Footbridge over brook.

high stile and cut diagonally across next field to stile and wooden footbridge. Keep ahead across next field and when you reach a **farm track**, bear left along it.

6 Just before you reach a gate, go obliquely right (through a 30 degree arc) and follow path across field, heading for **outbuildings** in the distance. Climb stile and proceed across shoulder of hill to another stile and footbridge. Cut across field towards outbuildings and garage, keeping hedgerow on your left. When you reach the field corner, go left through gate and then immediately right into woodland.

Cross **bridge** over canal (no.40) and then take the

Double Culvert Bridge (no. 40).

first left up flight of steps into woodland. Follow path through wood, with chocolate-coloured canal and wooded cutting on your left.

8 Pass two large beech trees in a clearing, where the bank falls away to your right, to give good views of **Loynton Moss** and its reed beds.

Beech trees near Loynton Moss.

Grub Street Cutting suffered regular landslips during construction due to friable rock strata. In 1834, 10,000 cubic yards of rock and marl came thundering down the walls of the cutting and blocked the canal (near Blakemere) for a distance of 60 yards.

9 Just before you reach the busy **A 519** (Newport to Eccleshall road) and the **High Bridge (no. 39)**, bear right along path, which runs parallel to the road. Descend flight of steps to a clearing and cross wooden footbridge with handrails on both sides. Go through gate and follow path across meadow to car park where the walk began.

8 Shebdon, Knighton and High Offley

A chocolate factory, a hilltop church and an award-winning pub are all on offer on this delightful 5 ½ mile circuit.

The Cadbury's factory at Knighton was in use between 1911 and 1961 and their fleet of horse-drawn narrow boats made regular collections of milk churns from local dairy farms. The milk was evaporated, added to cocoa-bean powder and sugar to produce 'chocolate crumb'. This partly processed chocolate kept well and was transported to Bournville, south Birmingham (a 15 hour journey by canal barge) to be made into Cadbury's 'Dairy Milk'.

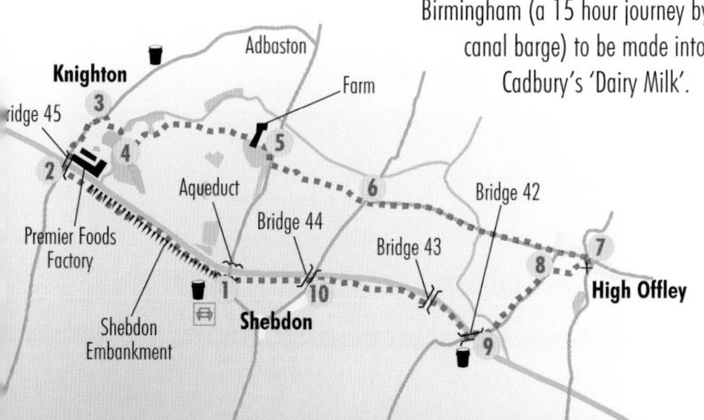

Level:
Length: 5 ½ miles (8.8 km)
Terrain: Easy walking along canal embankment and field paths. Some road walking involved, before regaining towpath.
Park and start: Layby near the Wharf Inn, Shebdon.
Start ref: SJ 758260
Postcode (nearest): ST20 0PY
Public transport: None to start, but Arriva bus 433 from Stafford to Woodseaves stops in Shebdon.
Refreshments and facilities: The Wharf Inn, Shebdon; The Haberdashers Arms, Knighton; The Anchor Inn, High Offley .

1 Walk up the ramp opposite the **Wharf Inn** and join the canal towpath at the **winding hole**. Bear left here and continue along the **Shebdon Embankment**, which carries the canal towards Knighton. Because of tree cover, it is sometimes difficult to appreciate just how high the canal is above the surrounding landscape.

A winding hole is a wider section of canal used as a turning point for 72 ft craft.

The Wharf Inn, Shebdon.

Shebdon Embankment.

2 After 1.5 km, there is a disused wharf, belonging to **Cadbury's dried milk factory**. The last cargo of 'chocolate crum' left here for Bournville in the early sixties. Continue under the **next bridge (no. 45)** and exit the canal via the steps

The Shebdon Embankment carries the canal northwards towards Knighton for over a mile, towering sixty feet above the surrounding fields.

Mallard and ducklings.

Cadbury's former factory and wharf.

Knighton (bridge 45).

The Premier Foods site at Knighton produces 29,000 tons of powder per annum, including Cadbury's Drinking Chocolate, Marvel and Birds Custard Powder.

provided. Gain the road and bear left past the **Premier Foods factory**.

3 Pass a lane on the left and then go right, after 100 metres, through a gate and across a sloping field towards a **large fishing lake**. Go clockwise round the lake, and over a low metal gate.

4 Bear left, soon afterwards, across a **footbridge** into an adjoining field, and then left along edge of field. Maintain direction when a broader track joins from the right and continue around perimeter of large field, as it swings round to the

Knighton fishing

right. Pass a copse on the left, where wood sorrel and celandine carpet the ground in spring. When the field ends, go through a gate and along the edge of a smaller field. Join a farm track, and ascend a small rise before passing **farm buildings** on the right. Climb a wooden gate and proceed along a tarred drive to a road.

5 Bear right along road and take the next left (opposite **Offley Grove**) along a bridleway. Continue along farm track, past two metal gates (which prevent vehicles from using this route as a short cut), until you reach a road.

6 Continue along road with no footway for 1.7 km, passing a farm on the left and **Peggs Lane** on the right, until you reach **St Mary's church, High Offley** and its clump of Scots pines.

High Offley church.

7 Go right through church gate and proceed to end of churchyard. From this vantage point, you can see the silvery thread of the **Shroppie** glinting in the sunlight and the conical outline of **The Wrekin**, wreathed in mist, on the distant horizon. Climb stile at end of churchyard and then go half left across sloping field (which may contain cattle).

Locate high stile in hedge and carefully climb down steps to road.

8 Bear left along lane past **Peggs Farm** and keep going until you reach a canal bridge (near the **Anchor Inn**).

9 Go left through gate to join canal towpath and then left

The isolated Anchor Inn is a canalside pub that has been run by the same family for over 100 years – with beer still fetched in jugs straight from the cellar. It has a camping site and gift shop and regularly features in the CAMRA good beer guide.

Narrow boats near Anchor Inn.

again under **bridge (no. 42)**. Continue along towpath, with a plethora of craft moored on opposite bank. Look back for a superb view of High Offley church perched on the hilltop.

10 Pass under a road **bridge (no. 44)** and keep going until you reach the **winding hole** at Shebdon Wharf. Go left here down ramp to return to the **Wharf Inn** and layby, where the walk began.

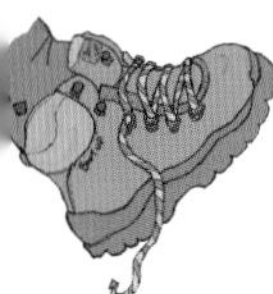

9 Goldstone and Cheswardine

A dramatic and unforgettable 6 mile hike along the Shroppie's deepest cutting and across miles of rolling farmland.

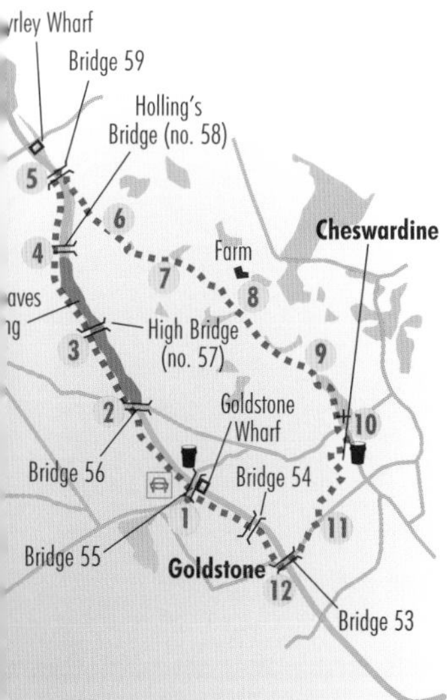

Hewn from solid sandstone without the benefit of mechanisation, Woodseaves Cutting is an astonishing memorial to the men who built the canal. The chasm-like cutting – around ninety feet deep – extends for over a mile between bridges 56 and 58, with ferns and mosses clinging to the sandstone walls and creepers trailing down. The contractor for this section, William Provis, faced enormous difficulties when he tried to cut through the crumbling sandstone in 1829.

Level:
Length: 6 miles (9.8 km)
Terrain: Towpath is muddy along wooded cutting and field paths are heavy going in places; walking boots essential.
Park and start: Layby near Goldstone Wharf (bridge 55); alternative parking at The Wharf Tavern (patrons only).
Start ref: SJ 705293
Postcode (nearest): TF9 2LP
Public transport: None to start, and infrequent bus services to Cheswardine.
Refreshments and facilities: The Wharf Tavern, Goldstone Wharf; pubs in Cheswardine (The Fox and Hounds; The Red Lion).

The Wharf Tavern, Goldstone.

1 Gain the canal at **Goldstone Wharf** (bridge 55) and bear left along towpath. Pass the **Wharf Tavern**, a caravan park and an overflow to the canal.

L.T.C. Rolt, made his 'dream-like' visit to the Wharf Tavern in 1939, and found: 'a cheerful fire blazing in the little bar parlour, where sat the landlord, his wife and the captain of the horse-boat with a pint glass on the table before him'.

2 Keep ahead under **bridge 56** (a road bridge) where the canal enters **Woodseaves** Cutting – one of the deepest on the Shroppie – with ferns and mosses clinging to the sandstone walls. The towpath here consists of flagstones, covered with moss, which can be slippy and uneven – so be careful! Continue past a pile of sandstone rocks, which appear to have crumbled away from the almost precipitous walls on the opposite bank. In winter, the landslips deposit red earth and rubble into the canal and towpath, and provide work for the British Waterways maintenance staff.

Woodseaves Cutting.

3 Pass under **High Bridge (no. 57)**, which soars high above the gorge, as the towpath starts to get wetter and muddier. The puddles that collect on the soggier sections, are a reddish sandstone colour. The tyre marks in the mud indicate that the path must get a fair amount of use, although it is certainly not as well maintained as the busier sections around Tyrley. When the canal swings

Cruising under High Bridge (no. 57)

L.T.C. Rolt describes his passage though Woodseaves Cutting in Narrow Boat*: 'Even the familiar canal bridges had here assumed strange and fanciful proportions, their arches airily heightened in their leap from lip to lip of the gorge'.*

to the right, in a slow sweeping arc, you can be assured that the worst of the mud is over, and that the path will get drier and more navigable, after the next bridge!

4 Pass under **Holling's Bridge (no. 58)**, which appears to have been reinforced in places, with black circular shields. Proceed along this rather eerie wooded section for

The remote Holling's Bridge (no. 58).

about 500 metres until the canal veers slightly left, past an overflow and the next **bridge (no. 59)** comes into view.

5 Leave the canal here via the ramp, and then go left over **bridge (no. 59)**. From here you can see craft moored between this bridge and **Tyrley Wharf** – and can breathe a sigh of relief that civilization is not far away. Continue through woodland and over a fence, then bear right along edge of field. Keep going until

you reach a wall, then follow it round to the left, and over a stile. Continue along wide walkway with giant elephant grass on both sides. It is likely that this crop – well over 6 feet tall – is being grown as a biofuel. And when the wind gets up, this fen-like landscape makes a roaring sound. Go over a wooden footbridge, then continue across another field of the same crop.

Elephant grass, can grow to the staggering height of 10 feet in one season, and is burnt as a 'carbon neutral' biofuel to produce heat and steam to power turbines.

6 Cross farm track and follow waymark post with yellow arrow, across a further field of the same crop. Pass an oak tree in the centre of the walkway, and then cross a footbridge into woodland. Cross two further footbridges before exiting woodland and proceed across another field of the same crop. At end of field, follow yellow arrow into sycamore woodland, and proceed along right hand edge of next field for about 100 metres.

7 Turn right at an easily-missed fingerpost into woodland and then swing left, past a pit, which marks the boundary of Staffordshire and Shropshire. Continue on path between two large holly bushes and along right hand edge of spinney. Proceed along right hand edge of next field, which can be heavy going, because of the long grass and uneven

Entering Haywood Drumble.

ground. Cross farm track and disconnect electric fencing using the orange insulated handles provided. Pass to the left of a small pit (with farm on left), then go through a metal gate at top of field. Continue along left hand edge of next field, and enter woodland **(Haywood Drumble)** via stile. Pass first pit and then bear left before second one, along path overgrown with ferns.

8 Exit this delightful patch of woodland via stile and proceed along right hand edge of next field. Disconnect electric fencing via orange insulated handle, and climb stile into woodland **(Lawn Drumble)**. Cross footbridge and climb stile to exit woodland. Keep ahead for ca. 50 metres and then bear half right along walkway with elephant grass on both sides.

Elephant grass near Lawn Drumble.

Wide skies near Cheswardine.

9 At end of field locate the double fingerpost and follow path into woodland. Pass holly bushes and chestnut trees, and when you reach a fallen tree, follow path as it swings right, through a horseshoe bend. At

Many of the navvies employed on the Shroppie were noted for their hard work, rough living and heavy drinking. They gained notoriety, around Cheswardine, for poaching and stealing hens' eggs.

St Swithun's Church, Cheswardine.

the next fork, branch left and follow rising path through woodland. When you reach an untarred lane, bear left along it, and keep going until you reach **St Swithun's church, Cheswardine**.

10 Turn left at T-junction, past the **Fox and Hounds pub**, and then go right along **Symons Way**. Follow road as it swings left into **Copelea**, past a green and a crescent of bungalows. Just before you reach a play area, turn right along a hedged track, with houses on the left. Go through gate at end of track and follow yellow waymark along right hand edge of field. **The Wrekin and Shropshire Hills** should now be visible on the distant horizon. Climb stile at end of field and then go left along edge of next field.

11 When you reach a road, bear right and follow it to a **canal bridge (no. 53)**.

Harvesting as storm clouds gather.

12 Turn right down ramp and maintain direction along towpath. Pass under **bridge 54** and exit canal at next **bridge (no. 55)**. Bear left along road to reach layby where the walk began.

10 Market Drayton and Tyrley Locks

A 4½ mile ramble that combines a flight of five locks hewn from solid sandstone with a market town steeped in history.

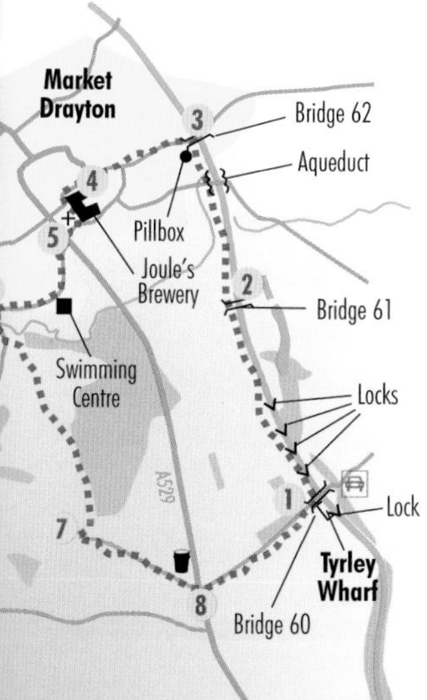

In 1245 the Cistercian monks of Combermere sought a market charter for the town from Henry III. It was the Spice Trade and the East India Company that summoned the young Robert Clive, the town's most famous son, to India at the age of seventeen. Then came gingerbread and the canal that Telford built, with its flight of five locks, to carry off all those market goods to the neighbouring towns.

Level:
Length: 4 ½ miles (7.3 km)
Terrain: Easy walking along canal tow-path through market town and along minor roads.
Park and start: Layby near Tyrley Wharf (bridge 60).
Start ref: SJ 690325
Postcode (nearest): TF9 2AH
Public transport: None to start, but Arriva 64 bus from Shrewsbury stops in Market Drayton.
Refreshments and facilities: The Four Alls Inn; pubs in Market Drayton (The Crown; The Talbot Inn).

Narrow boat emerging from Tyrley Locks.

Ferns thrive in the damp Tyrley Cutting.

(1) Gain the canal at **Tyrley Wharf** (bridge 60) – where the flight of five locks begins – and bear left along towpath. The **first lock**, opposite the wharf, is at the end of a 17 mile long pound – the previous lock being Wheaton Aston. After

Narrow boat approaching Tyrley Locks.

the **second** and **third locks**, a fast flowing channel joins the canal, on the far bank. After the **fourth lock**, the canal passes through a cutting with steep, sculptured sandstone walls. After the **fifth lock**, the cutting gets deeper and more dramatic, with ferns and mosses growing out of the sandstone. In due course, the banks get shallower and the canal gets nar-

Narrow section of 'cut' near Tyrley.

rower – so narrow that two boats find it difficult to pass. A milepost indicates that Nantwich is only 13 miles away from here!

Pass under **bridge 61**, where the canal widens out again and is about the same level as the surrounding land – but not for long! In due course, the canal crosses the Tern Valley on a lofty embankment, fringed with pine trees. If you come in summer, you may see Speckled Wood, Small Tortoiseshell and Peacock butterflies flying around. Cross **an aqueduct** over the **River Tern**, with forty stone steps leading to a road below. Proceed along a linear section of canal with craft moored on the towpath side.

To shorten journey times and improve efficiency, the locks on the Shroppie were purposely grouped into flights. The flight of five locks at Tyrley lowers the canal by 33 feet.

Narrow boat near bridge 61.

Looking down from bridge 62.

3 Leave the canal at the **next bridge (no. 62)**, taking a path off to the left, past a **concrete pillbox**. Bear left again when you reach the main road, and proceed past a playing field, barn conversions, an entrance to **Grove School** and the **Job Centre**, before reaching a mini roundabout.

4 Maintain direction past **Asda**, the **Stafford Court Hotel** and a number of quaint half-timbered buildings, until you reach the top of

Joule's Brewery, Market Drayton.

Gingerbread has been baked in Market Drayton for over two hundred years using traditional recipies, which are a closely guarded secret. Billington's, the oldest surviving brand, was first made here in 1817.

the High Street near **The Crown** pub. Follow road round to the left and keep to the left hand footpath along **Great Hales Street**. Cross road just before the **Joule's Brewery**, and follow footpath as it swings sharply to the right.

5 Leave the **A529 (to Newport)** at the next bend and keep ahead along a minor road. Cross road and follow path beside white railings past **Market Drayton**

Eleven year old Robert Clive (later Clive of India) came to Market Drayton in 1737, and acquired a daredevil reputation for climbing the church tower, sitting astride one of the gargoyles and taunting the townsfolk below.

The nation's 'favourite' yogurt, Müller, is manufactured at a state-of-the-art facility in Market Drayton. In 2001 the site was extended to create the largest yogurt factory in the UK.

Swimming Centre. This road follows the former route of the Müller 10K Road Race through Market Drayton. Cross to the right hand side of the road, just after a right hand bend and proceed along **Walkmill Road** and past a row of semi-detached houses.

6 Turn left (opposite **Red Bank**) and continue over bridge, past **NFU Mutual**. Take the next left along **Sandy Lane**, which is tarred at first, but then becomes untarred and increasingly sandy. Pass a huge chestnut tree and proceed on a rising path with fields on both sides. After passing houses on the left, the lane gets progressively steeper. Keep following bridleway over crest of hill and then round a right hand bend.

7 Follow track as it swings sharply left and merges with a tarred lane. Keep going past a cream-coloured farmhouse with numerous tractors in the grounds, until you reach the main road (near the **Four Alls Inn**).

Lock opposite Tyrley Wharf.

The Four Alls Inn.

8 Cross the busy **A529** and continue down lane to the layby (near **Tyrley Wharf**), where the walk began.